AFTERFEATHER

By
Black Bough Poetry

© Black Bough Poetry, 2022

All rights reserved; no part of this book may be reproduced by any means without the publisher's permission. Short extracts may be quoted on social media or reviews.

The authors have asserted their right to be identified as the authors of this work in accordance with the Copyright, Designs and Patents Act 1988.

Cover design by Alex Stevens.

Typeset by Briony Collins.

Edited by Briony Collins and Matthew M.C. Smith.

Guest Editor:

Working on this anthology is a dream realised. A brilliant press, phenomenal artist, and a selection of some of the finest poets I've ever encountered, all coming together in the pages of a single book to create something truly special. That is *Afterfeather*. The hours I poured into editing this did not feel like work but were instead spent in a state of unfiltered delight. For this joy, I must thank Matt for being Black Bough's generous and encouraging captain, who gave me this opportunity and many others through a press that my poetry-heart adores. I also owe the deepest gratitude to Alex Stevens for allowing us the gift of featuring his art here. Next, I leave this note with a wealth of admiration and respect to the poets within: for your magnificent talent, the riches of your craft, and the beautiful people you are – thank you. Last, to the reader, turn the page! Treasure awaits!

Briony Collins

General Editor:

When I looked at asking for a guest editor for an edition of Black Bough Poetry, my immediate thought was Briony Collins the award-winning, widely-published writer. Briony is a friend to this press with a dazzling series of poems published with us, all included in her online Silver Branch feature. Briony immediately agreed and requested artwork from Cardiff-based artist, Alex Stevens. In many ways, this summer 2022 edition, is more Black Bough than Black Bough – full of emotionally-loaded, vivid, short poems, electrified by Alex's visuals. Briony and Alex are a dream combination and we'd like to thank all poets for submitting and to those included. A great thing to feature Zoë Brigley and John McCullough; one of our shared goals to get their work in a Black Bough book! Huge thanks to Briony for putting this work together and Alex for such striking art.

Best,

Matthew M. C. Smith

Contents

3: The Sky Road Home, *Rhona Greene*

3: self contained, *Lynn Valentine*

4: June, *Letitia Jiju*

4: Sleep, *Jamie Woods*

5: Scree, *Marta Bílková*

7: Strawberries, *Louise Machen*

8: Expectation, *Helen Laycock*

9: Barren, *Thea Otípková*

9: The Chill, *Elizabeth Barton*

11: I haven't marked my days the right way, *Lee Potts*

11: The neocortex has a lot to answer for, *Ankh Spice*

12: And still…, *Alison Lock*

12: there is no colour without light, *Gerry Stewart*

13: Maiden Voyage, *Briony Collins*

15: How Gold they are, Before they Fall, *Anna Saunders*

15: Slowworm, *Louise Longson*

16: Sundial, *Vikki C.*

17: The Growl, *Roger Hare*

19: Horses, *John McCullough*

20: Hand and Hairpins, *Zoë Brigley*

21: Wellspring, *Oormila Vijayakrishnan Prahlad*

23: Aurora Magic, *Matthew M.C. Smith*

23: In Hollow Copse, *Laura Hemmington*

24: On a Summer Morning, *Merril D. Smith*

25: Biographies

28: Recommended Reading

AFTERFEATHER

Content Warning:

Please be aware that some of the poems in *Afterfeather* discuss sensitive topics, such as miscarriage, stillbirth, infertility, death, and grief.

The Sky Road Home

Walked up the long gone
avenue to my old gone
long-ago school. Found myself – there – under
the chestnut tree, behind the bicycle shed – rusty, skeletal remains
fallen horse chestnut brown time-forgotten deep buried
relics. Resurrected a little russet-red conker-headbanger girl.
'Whose child is this?' wheezed the unsettled
breeze that rattled and shook the shivering leaves still
clinging to an imperceptible line of invisible
trees uncast at last from their long dark shadows.
'She's mine!' I exclaimed and reclaimed myself. Light
as a feather unfalling to bird, we took the sky
road home - together. Feather, afterfeather.

– *Rhona Greene*

        self   contained

    an unsettling   in the hawthorn bush
    a winter wind   rips at spring
      white petals

violated

    grass too long   in the churned up lawn
    roses clenched   anxious in their own heads
      by the wall   another dead rabbit
    lost to a virus   or fall of poison
      body slack   eyes locked on sky
      rooks arrive   a bicker of wings
        pick over   gristle veins
  a line of pines lean   on hills unmoving

– *Lynn Valentine*

June*

Meenachil scintillates
a cricket-sung silence.
I sing back.

We ashen
into rain,
ividey —

              here
we refract,
                   here
      strewn in the lone dimple
      of god's smile,

avidey —
we meet   again.
Everywhere.

      – Letitia Jiju

> *Malayalam word translations:*
>
> Meenachil – the arterial river of the district of Kottayam in Kerala
>
> Ividey – here
> Avidey – there

Sleep

Just boys stabbing at buzzing guitars, wielded semi-automatic,
cigarette smoke shimmers, auraed with lava-lamp desperation,

until daylight breaks, enters through summoning curtains, dust
mote beacons, white chrysanthemums and murderous birdsong
weaponized,

a broadsword swipes flatly, sharp rays poison and pollinate,
prising apart the shielding fingers, expose my naked streaming

eyes, and grief chisels my cindered heart again:
he was alive in my dream.

      – Jamie Woods

Scree

The dry crunch of
granite fracturing,

The sparkling outrage
in marmot's scream,

After hours
of climbing up stones
unturned,

Have you heard it too?
Sun ravened the world and
I have lost

to your silence.

Below this one last rock restrained
with steel cables, iron rungs,

Seeing you grasp at it,
Seeing how

terribly
it holds.

– Marta Bílková

i wish there was nothing i could do

Strawberries

The strawberry plants that flowered in spring
have been wiped out in this morning's storm

along with the garden fence and the tiny
cloche they were housed in.

I can't help thinking they'll be nothing for breakfast
and I don't want to go home.

This coffee tastes cheap and the concern
of strangers is unsettling.

I have my clothing in a sealed bag but no reply
to my messages. They tell me I'm free to leave

when all I'm left with are bloodstained jeans
and this lonely bus ride.

– Louise Machen

Expectation

Curled in a seashell
sunk in my skin,
you hear my heart surge.

Away from the swell,
you dwell,
   a membrane away

from the salt-lash,
the splintered wrist-pull
into soft wreckage.

You pale,
unfurled
in the wash of the waiting world;

frail waves splash:
cool you
blue.

        – Helen Laycock

Barren

In the end the winter always
moves inside, tired of its own cold.
It settles on chrome and glass,
in porcelain bowls. Behind mirrors.
Not often now but still,
she grows unexpectant,
which is when she tightropes
mothers' watchful stares in parks,
and falls and lands
on children's voices.
At home she lights a fire,
its glow eating through the dark,
swallowing
the chill.

– Radka Thea Otípková

The Chill

An icepick cleaves my back
breaking my bones of ice;
chill fire-flash reverberates
in every pondered movement,
every step a blow in the ancient
guarded snowpacked wasteland
that has become my body;
I am a snowdrift today, slow
as the world's turning, a cold sphere
holding a core burning in veins
hot tipped to my skin, fevered ice
jarring nerves like lava seeking
the cool surface of snows,
inching defiant, hacked chill
to the precipice of muffled blows
hurtling in the thunder of my head.

– Elizabeth Barton

minimum viable product 3

I haven't marked my days the right way

It's like I only managed to twist together bits
of yarn and thread picked out of my old clothes
and blankets, scorched and acrid, into cords
just to knot off each full moon. I counted months
and years of those fat, pitted stones cast over
the ocean's edge and all I have are numbers.
I know how many full moons, Masses skipped,
bottles of red wine, lawns cut, broken locks,
borrowed beds but I have no sketch books
or photos and the words I said and heard were tossed
into the compost like the bitter skin of an orange.
But I can't stop looking back and my fingers
are nicked and raw and sting from trying to hold on.

– Lee Potts

The neocortex has a lot to answer for

Sun halfway through her dizzy life—
only yesterday the great hoot
expanded to cradle a notion
waxed so giant. By treadle and by jaw
each bone box creaks awake, echoing
with terror at its own capacity.
And through canopy's dapple, the sun just nods
and continues to palm-and-drop the same soft,
bright leaves. *Ah, look up.*
This for you, baffled little ape. And this.
Mobile light, entranced pupil, once beneath this
we were branch-sway. Once she was the only watchfire
we had, once her estranged mother-dark rocked us kindly
and we nested dumb and unalone and ripe stars fell
freely into our unworded mouths
and we thought nothing—
not one thing of it.

– Ankh Spice

And still...

by sea-spewn waste
        reek of salt

bright glow buoys
        watch surfers

ride the outlet
        slack-sheet boats

wait by bleached jetties
        empty creels

piled on neon-waves
        litter rattles

a slipway as we yawn
        the deepest blues

lace-petals
        on a porcelain sky.

      – Alison Lock

there is no colour without light
falling light - painting by jenny mclaren

        smirr
    straight shiver of silver
down the spine   pine-threaded
     a mountain cup
filled with the hush   rushing stand-still
       sparks of rain
   break the thrall   shawl of gray
     thrown over the loch
   smudged pale   exhale

        – Gerry Stewart

Maiden Voyage *(excerpt)*

The longboat shudders its keel
        rears itself to cut the wave
                A raven sits on the bow

                    Hrafn?

                        with its oil-spill feathers
                  beak hooked to fish directions
            from a night as thin as wind

      Hrafn?

blinks cut into salt dark
        rheum gathering in corners
                eclipsed by a membrane

                      Hrafn?

                        I steer this vessel
            moon-starched epidermis and fatty tissue
        But these waters are new

what am I

        what   are   I

                    our eyes black as beaches
                a creature calling
        oh gods   *define me*

— *Briony Collins*

minimum viable product 2

How Gold they are, Before they Fall

In the last days of his life
my father lay on his bed, slender as a sapling.

All through his illness, he was rooted to home,
his energy slowly seeping out.

How luminous he was, in his late season,
his eyes beatific.

The leaves look radiant
as they hang above the dark earth.

How gold they are, before they fall.

– *Anna Saunders*

Slowworm

finding you
under the sun-
weighted stone; molten-bright
gold and patinated bronze scales-
the unalloyed
wonder

– *Louise Longson*

Sundial

We planted light in late summer
the kind that falls unannounced
a pale blossom on bare shoulders
rain sliding off the statues of a lost era

how the sky took us to seed, fists unfurling
as if fearless of a sundial antiquated with shadows
my collarbone collecting it all for the tiny birds
your eyes perfecting the art of Elysium

a flood spilling over, as it must
bright peonies protesting all my wars
marigolds as peace signs on every corner
the scent of mercy, in the garden

the bouquet I saved for the end
when fields were fallow, doors bolted,
watching from the annex, windows misted
your distant body, a god shaped cloud

along the arched spine of Polzeath bay,
gloaming, a plum, bruised in your palm
to have it all, stained with the injuries of a full life
oh…how the storm keeps coming.

– Vikki C.

The Growl

prises apart the muscles and mucosa
of livid vocal cords, rakes the air
into migraines that wrack a resting grin
into a rictus to release it,
to pluck its claws on my malleus,
incus and stapes, to trace
blood's flow beneath
the thin skin of my civility.

The growl burns behind the hound's eyes, deep
in a cave in a cliff in a company of fur
that learned to be heard
by rock and wraith alike.
My shadow rises
but cannot withstand the dark song,
retreats and slips from the edge to leave me
clinging to the lip of a precipice
by the untutored fingertips of my longing.

– Roger Hare

Arrange your life in order to attract predators

Horses

Now I'm a cricket, I hide in Gertrude Stein's cuckoo clock, waiting to sing.

I'm a deviant falling from the roof of a car park.

Lonely, I get bladdered with Sappho and dance.

I'm the plumber who leaves a floater in Thatcher's toilet.

Clubbed in a police cell, my sandcastle face crumbles.

A handkerchief in Claude McKay's breast pocket, I thrill beside his riotous heart.

I can never express all of myself at once, the hole of me.

I hunt my scattered names but the past wears ice skates, keeps curving about.

When I die on Brighton Pier, the carousel organ will stop, the gilded horse I'm slumped on will vanish.

Secretly, I'll still be riding full pelt.

– John McCullough

Hand and Hairpins

Dear Stieglitz –

Remember the photograph
    you took from behind –

                      my
           hand pinning hair for the
               flash of neck
         and shoulders bare – the white
              tips of my fairy
        ears – & you even caught
              the Pleiades on
      the side of my face. There –
              the view you saw each day

& here your own fingers
    – twisting the hair to a stump.

    – Zoë Brigley

Wellspring

Songbirds ricochet off
the midday firmament.

sand tempests snuff breath—
sacs of shriveled alveoli.

She levitates into the ether,
mellow mother-goddess

smoothing the foil
of inclement skies.

Vengeful suns dwindle—
oases open in her palms,

as aviaries of finches stir,
beaks agape, thirsting for

her emerald waters
amniotic wellspring—

maternal mercy.

– Oormila Vijayakrishnan Prahlad

the sex and diet of dead things

Aurora Magic

Only once we caught fluorescent
flashes of the Northern lights,
beyond the bite of the Great Bear's
diamonds; a ghoulish spectre under
hailing starlight. We were there,
our fingers tangled, smooth flesh
over bones crossed. We looked on,
eyes wide, glimpsing aurora; our souls
as spectres in brief brilliance. And there,
the mountains fell to the east, to dawn's
far region where fields of frost
blind the eyes of the waking god.
We were there, alive and one.

– *Matthew M.C. Smith*

In Hollow Copse

Late solstice sun —
day descending soft
to needle peppered gorge
where comet tails make
double helix
burnished coppers
click and burr

– *Laura Hemmington*

On a Summer Morning

I watch the osprey fly, bobble-winged
she dives beak first through reflected clouds,
white sheets hanging on the river's surface,

plunging like joy, to rise in hope
with iridescent-scaled prize, a rainbow carried
into a sky of blueberries and cream,

now crow-chatter, robin trill, and a cardinal's red flash,
remind me of the hour, I walk toward the sun and you, home.

> *– Merril D. Smith*

Biographies

The *Afterfeather* Team

Briony Collins is the author of *Blame it on Me* and *All That Glisters*, both published by Broken Sleep Books. Her next instalment of poetry – *The Birds, The Rabbits, The Trees* – is forthcoming with them in April 2023. Currently, Briony manages her time between running *Cape Magazine* and working on her PhD. Website: www.brionycollins.co.uk / Twitter: @ri_collins

Alex Stevens is a mixed-media artist living in Cardiff. Using references from anatomy, zoology, and biology, he attempts to make images that shred the veil between magic and science, dream and nightmare, the mundane and the uncanny. His work has appeared in a variety of publications, including Steel Incisors, Penteract Press, The Ghastling, and WyrdDaze. Twitter: @abjectobjects / Instagram: @abject_objects

Matthew M.C. Smith is a 'Best of the Net' nominated writer from Swansea with work in Poetry Wales, The Lonely Crowd and Broken Spine. He is editor on Twitter of @TopTweetTuesday and @blackboughpoems. Twitter: @MatthewMCSmith

---

Rhona Greene is an avid poetry fan and accidental emerging writer from Dublin delighted to be published with Black Bough Poetry in their Freedom-Rapture anthology and Christmas /Winter editions Vol. 2 & 3 and online @sacosw Advent Poems 2021. She's thrilled to be in this special Summer edition. Twitter: @Rhona_Greene

Lynn Valentine lives in the Scottish Highlands. Her debut collection, *Life's Stink and Honey*, was published by Cinnamon Press in 2022, after winning the Cinnamon Literature Award. Her Scots language pamphlet, *A Glimmer o Stars*, was published by Hedgehog Poetry Press in 2021, after winning their dialect competition. Twitter: @dizzylynn

Letitia Jiju has a penchant for imagist poems and retelling the divine & the mythological. Her poems have appeared/are forthcoming in Zero Readers, Amethyst Review, Moist Poetry Journal, Acropolis Journal and Emirates Literature Festival. She serves as Poetry Editor at Mag 20/20. You can find her on Instagram/Twitter @eaturlettuce

Jamie Woods is a writer from Swansea, with poems in *Poetry Wales, Ink Sweat & Tears* and *Spoonie Journal,* and fiction in *Evergreen Review* and *The Lonely Crowd*. He is poet-in-residence at the charity Leukaemia Care, and was commended in the Hippocrates International Prize for Poetry and Medicine 2021. Website: www.jamiewoods77.com / Twitter: @JamieWoods77

Marta Bílková is a logician and poet from Prague, Czechia, writing in Czech and English. She has been a finalist of Básně SK/CZ 2021, with her collection of twelve poems published in the competition volume. Occasional photographer and graphic arts lover, she aims to make it all work together eventually. Twitter: @MartaBilkova

Louise Machen is a Mancunian poet and a graduate of The Centre for New Writing at The University of Manchester. Her poetry likes to explore relationships through narrative and visual detail and has most recently appeared in *Grand Little Things, The Olney Magazine, Forge Zine* and *Full House Literary*. Twitter: @LouLouMach

Helen Laycock is a poet and storyteller. Her writing has appeared at *Reflex Fiction*, the *Ekphrastic Review, Cabinet of Heed, Visual Verse, Paragraph Planet, Serious Flash Fiction, Flash Flood, Popshot, Lucent Dreaming, Full Moon and Foxglove, The Caterpillar*, et al. She is currently compiling themed poetry collections and a second volume of microfiction. Twitter: @helen_laycock

Radka Thea Otípková's first language is Czech, but she writes poetry exclusively in English. In 2019 she won the Waltham Forest Poetry Competition. Her poems have appeared online in B O D Y and Moria and in print in The North and Tears in the Fence. Twitter: @thea_otipkova

Elizabeth Barton is a poet and artist from New Zealand with work featured in various online journals including Fevers of the Mind, Amphora, The Hyacinth Review, as well as the anthologies Vita Brevis Press: Nothing Divine Dies, Black Bough Poetry's Rapture: Dark Confessions and Winter/Christmas Edition 2021. A winner of the White Label Cinq poetry competition in 2020, she has a collection soon to be published with Hedgehog Poetry Press. Twitter: @DestinyAngel25

Lee Potts, author of the chapbook *And Drought Will Follow* (Frosted Fire, 2021), is poetry editor at *Barren Magazine*. His work has appeared in *The Night Heron Barks, Rust + Moth, Whale Road Review, UCity Review, Firmament, Moist Poetry Journal*, and elsewhere. He lives just outside of Philadelphia. Twitter: @LeePottsPoet

Ankh Spice is an Aotearoa New Zealand poet, author of *The Water Engine* (Femme Salvé Books, 2021). His prize-winning poetry is widely published, eight times nominated for Pushcart Prize/Best of the Net. He's a poetry contributing editor at Barren Magazine and co-edits at IceFloe Press. Website: www.ankhspice-seagoatscreamspoetry.com / Twitter: @SeaGoatScreamsPoetry / Facebook: @AnkhSpiceSeaGoatScreamsPoetry

Alison Lock's poetry, fiction, and non-fiction has been published widely. Her poetry collections are: *A Slither of Air* (2011), *Beyond Wings* (2015), *Revealing the Odour of Earth* (2017). *Lure* (2020), broadcast on Radio 3, and, most recently, *Unfurling* (2022) – a sequence written as a response to the lockdown. Website: www.alisonlock.com / Twitter: @alilock4

Gerry Stewart is a poet, creative writing tutor and editor based in Finland. Her poetry collection Post-Holiday Blues was published by Flambard Press, UK. Caledonian Antisyzygy is to be published by Hedgehog Poetry Press in 2022. Writing blog: http://thistlewren.blogspot.fi/ / Twitter: @grimalkingerry

Anna Saunders is the author of *Communion*, (Wild Conversations Press), *Struck*, (Pindrop Press) *Kissing the She Bear*, (Wild Conversations Press), *Burne Jones and the Fox* (Indigo Dreams) *Ghosting for Beginners* (Indigo Dreams), and *Feverfew* (Indigo Dreams). Anna is the CEO and founder of Cheltenham Poetry Festival. Twitter: @AnnaSaund1

Louise Longson started writing in her late 50s, during isolation in lockdown 2020 and has since been widely published in print and online. She is the author of chapbooks *Hanging Fire* (Dreich Publications, 2021) and *Songs from the Witch Bottle: cytoplasmic variations* (Alien Buddha Press, 2022). Twitter: @LouisePoetical

Vikki C. is a British born poet and fiction writer whose work features vivid imagery inspired by the themes of existentialism, science and nature. Her writing has been published in several anthologies. She is also a spoken word artist, pianist and composer. Twitter: @VWC_Writes

Roger Hare writes from a love of being diverted by an idea, something overheard, an observation, insight or emotion and the stimulation offered by works of art. He's published in several online/in-print magazines and anthologies, is a two-time competition prizewinner and Pushcart nominated in 2021. Twitter: @RogerHare6

John McCullough's book of poems, *Reckless Paper Birds* (Penned in the Margins) won the 2020 Hawthornden Prize for Literature and was shortlisted for the Costa Poetry Award. His new collection, *Panic Response*, includes 'Flower of Sulphur', shortlisted for the 2021 Forward Prize for Best Single Poem. He lives in Hove. Twitter: @JohnMcCullough_

Zoë Brigley is a Welsh-American writer with three award winning collections of poetry from Bloodaxe and a book of nonfiction essays. She is editor of *Poetry Wales*, a poetry editor at Seren Books, and works at the Ohio State University. She edited *100 Poems to Save the Earth* (Seren 2021). Website: www.zoebrigley.com / Twitter: @ZoeBrigley

Oormila Vijayakrishnan Prahlad is an Indian-Australian artist, poet, and improv pianist. Her art and poetry have been published in various journals and anthologies including *Eunoia Review, Cordite Poetry Review, Bracken Magazine*, and *Black Bough Poetry*. Twitter: @oormilaprahlad / Instagram: @oormila_paintings

Laura Hemmington is a writer and freelance copywriter who recently left London for the Isle of Wight. Her poems have appeared in Crab Creek Review, Visual Verse, Emerge, and No Contact. Twitter: @laurahemmington

Merril D. Smith lives and writes in southern New Jersey near the Delaware River. Her poetry has been published in previous issues of Black Bough Poetry as well as in other journals. Her full-length collection, *River Ghosts*, was published by Nightingale and Sparrow Press. Twitter: @merril_mds

Recommended Reading

Community is the lifeblood of poetry. Continue your support by checking out some of Black Bough's friends.

Books:
Blame it on Me – Briony Collins (Broken Sleep, 2021)
All That Glisters – Briony Collins (Broken Sleep, 2022)
Origin: 21 Poems – Matthew M.C. Smith (Amazon, 2018)
Under Photon Crowns – Dai Fry (Black Bough, 2021)
Deep Time Vol. 1 (Black Bough, 2020)
Deep Time Vol. 2 (Black Bough, 2020)
Christmas & Winter Vol. 1 (Black Bough, 2020)
Christmas & Winter Vol. 2 (Black Bough, 2021)
Dark Confessions (Black Bough, 2021)
Freedom-Rapture (Black Bough, 2021)

Forthcoming:
The Birds, The Rabbits, The Trees – Briony Collins (Broken Sleep, 2023)
Nights on the Line – M.S. Evans (Black Bough, 2022)
(Title TBA) – Matthew M.C. Smith (The Broken Spine, 2022)
Christmas & Winter Vol. 3 (Black Bough, 2022)

Presses:
Cape Magazine (https://capemagazineteam.wixsite.com/mysite)
Poetry Wales (https://poetrywales.co.uk/)
Broken Sleep Books (https://www.brokensleepbooks.com/)
The Broken Spine (https://thebrokenspine.co.uk/)
Barren Magazine (https://barrenmagazine.com/)

Printed in Great Britain
by Amazon